MW01242049

CREATIVE CONFIDENT PAPER CO.
Pet Records

IN CASE OF LOSS, PLEASE RETURN TO:

_____

_____

_____

_____

Important Phone Numbers

Veterinarian

Emergency Vet

Groomer

Animal Shelter

Animal Control

Local Relative

Pet Friendly Neighbor

ASPCA Animal Poison Control Center
888-426-4435
If you think your pet may have ingested a potentially poisonous substance, you can call this poison control center 24 hours a day, 365 days a year. The cost for a poison-related emergency consultation with a veterinarian or toxicologist is $65, which can be billed to your credit card.

Pet Poison Hotline
888-426-4435
This 24-hour animal poison control service for the U.S., Canada, and the Caribbean charges a $35 per incident fee, payable by credit card. This fee covers the initial consultation as well as all follow-up calls associated with the management of the case.

Spay/USA Helpline
800-248-7729
This national spay/neuter referral service can help you find a low-cost clinic in your area. Their mission is to reduce pet overpopulation by making spay/neuter services affordable to everyone who has a cat or a dog. Phone counselors are available M-F from 9 a.m. to 4:30 p.m. EST.

The Animal Legal Defense Fund
707-795-2533
The nonprofit ALDF was founded in 1979 by attorneys active in shaping the emerging field of animal law. Contact them if you have questions about animal neglect or abuse, pet related landlord-tenant issues, pet

custody concerns during a divorce, or if you need information on how to include animals in your will.

ASPCA Pet Loss Hotline
877-474-3310
This program was created to help pet owners who are dealing with the loss of a pet. You can also call them for assistance with the decision to euthanize, advice on how to help children, disabled individuals and other family pets who are grieving the loss of their companion, and help establishing a relationship with a new pet.

Pet Travel Information
877-241-0184
If you're planning to travel with your pet by plane, train or cruise ship, call Pettravel.com for information on regulations and restrictions, pet container requirements, vet certificates, and clearing security.

Pet Airways
888-738-2479
The world's first pet-only airline currently transports four-legged passengers between nine major U.S. cities, with several more in the works.

Animal Behavior Hotline
312-644-8338, ext. 343
Behavior specialists are available to answer questions and provide solutions on everything from separation anxiety to aggression.

Lyme Disease Foundation
860-870-0070
The LDF is a nonprofit organization dedicated to finding solutions for tick borne disorders. Call them if you need information on tick-borne diseases such as Lyme Disease, Rocky Mountain Spotted Fever and Colorado Tick Fever.

Stolen Pet Hotline
800-STOLEN-PET
The Stolen Pet Hotline is the number to call if you think that your pet has been stolen. When a dog disappears, it can be a traumatic experience and you do not want to think that someone may have taken your pet. This hotline exists to offer assistance if you think your dog has been stolen.

Owner Details

OWNER 1

Name

Address

City

State

Postal Code

Phone Number

OWNER 2

Name

Address

City

State

Postal Code

Phone Number

OWNER 3

Name

Address

City

State

Postal Code

Phone Number

Pet Details

Photo of Pet

Name

Microchip ID

Species

Breed

Sex

Date of Birth

Color

Markings and
Distinguishing
Features

Responds To

Vaccinations

DATE	AGE	TYPE OF VACCINE	BATCH NUMBER	GIVEN BY	EXPIRES

Vaccinations

DATE	AGE	TYPE OF VACCINE	BATCH NUMBER	GIVEN BY	EXPIRES

Vet Visit Log

Date

Age

Kind of Visit   ◯ Routine   ◯ Emergency

Reason for
Visit

Shots

Medication

Other
Treatment

Comments

Vet Visit Log

Date

Age

Kind of Visit   ◯ Routine   ◯ Emergency

Reason for
Visit

Shots

Medication

Other
Treatment

Comments

Vet Visit Log

Date

Age

Kind of Visit   ◯ Routine   ◯ Emergency

Reason for
Visit

Shots

Medication

Other
Treatment

Comments

Vet Visit Log

Date

Age

Kind of Visit   ◯ Routine   ◯ Emergency

Reason for
Visit

Shots

Medication

Other
Treatment

Comments

Vet Visit Log

Date

Age

Kind of Visit   ◯ Routine   ◯ Emergency

Reason for
Visit

Shots

Medication

Other
Treatment

Comments

Vet Visit Log

Date

Age

Kind of Visit ◯ Routine   ◯ Emergency

Reason for
Visit

Shots

Medication

Other
Treatment

Comments

Vet Visit Log

Date

Age

Kind of Visit ◯ Routine ◯ Emergency

Reason for
Visit

Shots

Medication

Other
Treatment

Comments

Vet Visit Log

Date

Age

Kind of Visit   ⭕ Routine   ⭕ Emergency

Reason for
Visit

Shots

Medication

Other
Treatment

Comments

Vet Visit Log

Date

Age

Kind of Visit   ◯ Routine   ◯ Emergency

Reason for
Visit

Shots

Medication

Other
Treatment

Comments

Vet Visit Log

Date

Age

Kind of Visit ⭘ Routine ⭘ Emergency

Reason for
Visit

Shots

Medication

Other
Treatment

Comments

Vet Visit Log

Date

Age

Kind of Visit   ◯ Routine   ◯ Emergency

Reason for
Visit

Shots

Medication

Other
Treatment

Comments

Vet Visit Log

Date

Age

Kind of Visit   ◯ Routine   ◯ Emergency

Reason for
Visit

Shots

Medication

Other
Treatment

Comments

Vet Visit Log

Date

Age

Kind of Visit   ◯ Routine   ◯ Emergency

Reason for
Visit

Shots

Medication

Other
Treatment

Comments

Vet Visit Log

Date

Age

Kind of Visit   ◯ Routine   ◯ Emergency

Reason for
Visit

Shots

Medication

Other
Treatment

Comments

Vet Visit Log

Date

Age

Kind of Visit   ◯ Routine   ◯ Emergency

Reason for
Visit

Shots

Medication

Other
Treatment

Comments

Vet Visit Log

Date

Age

Kind of Visit   ◯ Routine   ◯ Emergency

Reason for
Visit

Shots

Medication

Other
Treatment

Comments

Vet Visit Log

Date

Age

Kind of Visit   ○ Routine   ○ Emergency

Reason for
Visit

Shots

Medication

Other
Treatment

Comments

Vet Visit Log

Date

Age

Kind of Visit   ◯ Routine   ◯ Emergency

Reason for
Visit

Shots

Medication

Other
Treatment

Comments

Vet Visit Log

Date

Age

Kind of Visit   ◯ Routine   ◯ Emergency

Reason for
Visit

Shots

Medication

Other
Treatment

Comments

Pet Details

Photo of Pet

Name

Microchip ID

Species

Breed

Sex

Date of Birth

Color

Markings and
Distinguishing
Features

Responds To

Vaccinations

DATE	AGE	TYPE OF VACCINE	BATCH NUMBER	GIVEN BY	EXPIRES

Vaccinations

DATE	AGE	TYPE OF VACCINE	BATCH NUMBER	GIVEN BY	EXPIRES

Vet Visit Log

Date

Age

Kind of Visit   ◯ Routine   ◯ Emergency

Reason for
Visit

Shots

Medication

Other
Treatment

Comments

Vet Visit Log

Date

Age

Kind of Visit   ◯ Routine   ◯ Emergency

Reason for
Visit

Shots

Medication

Other
Treatment

Comments

Vet Visit Log

Date

Age

Kind of Visit   ◯ Routine   ◯ Emergency

Reason for
Visit

Shots

Medication

Other
Treatment

Comments

Vet Visit Log

Date

Age

Kind of Visit ◯ Routine ◯ Emergency

Reason for
Visit

Shots

Medication

Other
Treatment

Comments

Vet Visit Log

Date

Age

Kind of Visit   ⃝   Routine   ⃝   Emergency

Reason for
Visit

Shots

Medication

Other
Treatment

Comments

Vet Visit Log

Date
_____

Age
_____

Kind of Visit   ◯ Routine   ◯ Emergency
_____

Reason for
Visit

_____

Shots

_____

Medication

_____

Other
Treatment

_____

Comments

Vet Visit Log

Date

Age

Kind of Visit   ○ Routine   ○ Emergency

Reason for
Visit

Shots

Medication

Other
Treatment

Comments

Vet Visit Log

Date

Age

Kind of Visit   ◯ Routine   ◯ Emergency

Reason for
Visit

Shots

Medication

Other
Treatment

Comments

Vet Visit Log

Date

Age

Kind of Visit   ◯ Routine   ◯ Emergency

Reason for
Visit

Shots

Medication

Other
Treatment

Comments

Vet Visit Log

Date

Age

Kind of Visit   ◯ Routine   ◯ Emergency

Reason for
Visit

Shots

Medication

Other
Treatment

Comments

Vet Visit Log

Date

Age

Kind of Visit   ◯ Routine   ◯ Emergency

Reason for
Visit

Shots

Medication

Other
Treatment

Comments

Vet Visit Log

Date

Age

Kind of Visit   ◯ Routine   ◯ Emergency

Reason for
Visit

Shots

Medication

Other
Treatment

Comments

Vet Visit Log

Date

Age

Kind of Visit   ◯ Routine   ◯ Emergency

Reason for
Visit

Shots

Medication

Other
Treatment

Comments

Vet Visit Log

Date

Age

Kind of Visit   ◯ Routine   ◯ Emergency

Reason for
Visit

Shots

Medication

Other
Treatment

Comments

Vet Visit Log

Date

Age

Kind of Visit   ◯   Routine   ◯   Emergency

Reason for
Visit

Shots

Medication

Other
Treatment

Comments

Vet Visit Log

Date

Age

Kind of Visit   ◯ Routine   ◯ Emergency

Reason for
Visit

Shots

Medication

Other
Treatment

Comments

Vet Visit Log

Date

Age

Kind of Visit   ◯ Routine   ◯ Emergency

Reason for
Visit

Shots

Medication

Other
Treatment

Comments

Vet Visit Log

Date

Age

Kind of Visit   ○ Routine   ○ Emergency

Reason for
Visit

Shots

Medication

Other
Treatment

Comments

Vet Visit Log

Date

Age

Kind of Visit   ◯ Routine   ◯ Emergency

Reason for
Visit

Shots

Medication

Other
Treatment

Comments

Pet Details

Photo of Pet

Name

Microchip ID

Species

Breed

Sex

Date of Birth

Color

Markings and
Distinguishing
Features

Responds To

Vaccinations

DATE	AGE	TYPE OF VACCINE	BATCH NUMBER	GIVEN BY	EXPIRES

Vaccinations

DATE	AGE	TYPE OF VACCINE	BATCH NUMBER	GIVEN BY	EXPIRES

Vet Visit Log

Date

Age

Kind of Visit   ◯ Routine   ◯ Emergency

Reason for
Visit

Shots

Medication

Other
Treatment

Comments

Vet Visit Log

Date

Age

Kind of Visit   ○ Routine   ○ Emergency

Reason for
Visit

Shots

Medication

Other
Treatment

Comments

Vet Visit Log

Date

Age

Kind of Visit   ◯ Routine   ◯ Emergency

Reason for
Visit

Shots

Medication

Other
Treatment

Comments

Vet Visit Log

Date

Age

Kind of Visit   ⚪ Routine   ⚪ Emergency

Reason for
Visit

Shots

Medication

Other
Treatment

Comments

Vet Visit Log

Date

Age

Kind of Visit   ◯ Routine   ◯ Emergency

Reason for
Visit

Shots

Medication

Other
Treatment

Comments

Vet Visit Log

Date

Age

Kind of Visit ◯ Routine ◯ Emergency

Reason for
Visit

Shots

Medication

Other
Treatment

Comments

Vet Visit Log

Date

Age

Kind of Visit   ◯ Routine   ◯ Emergency

Reason for
Visit

Shots

Medication

Other
Treatment

Comments

Vet Visit Log

Date

Age

Kind of Visit ◯ Routine ◯ Emergency

Reason for
Visit

Shots

Medication

Other
Treatment

Comments

Vet Visit Log

Date

Age

Kind of Visit   ○ Routine   ○ Emergency

Reason for
Visit

Shots

Medication

Other
Treatment

Comments

Vet Visit Log

Date

Age

Kind of Visit ○ Routine ○ Emergency

Reason for
Visit

Shots

Medication

Other
Treatment

Comments

Vet Visit Log

Date

Age

Kind of Visit   ◯ Routine   ◯ Emergency

Reason for
Visit

Shots

Medication

Other
Treatment

Comments

Vet Visit Log

Date

Age

Kind of Visit   ◯ Routine   ◯ Emergency

Reason for
Visit

Shots

Medication

Other
Treatment

Comments

Vet Visit Log

Date

Age

Kind of Visit ⚪ Routine ⚪ Emergency

Reason for
Visit

Shots

Medication

Other
Treatment

Comments

Vet Visit Log

Date

Age

Kind of Visit   ◯   Routine   ◯   Emergency

Reason for
Visit

Shots

Medication

Other
Treatment

Comments

Vet Visit Log

Date

Age

Kind of Visit   ◯ Routine   ◯ Emergency

Reason for
Visit

Shots

Medication

Other
Treatment

Comments

Vet Visit Log

Date

Age

Kind of Visit   ◯ Routine   ◯ Emergency

Reason for
Visit

Shots

Medication

Other
Treatment

Comments

Vet Visit Log

Date

Age

Kind of Visit   ◯ Routine   ◯ Emergency

Reason for
Visit

Shots

Medication

Other
Treatment

Comments

Vet Visit Log

Date

Age

Kind of Visit ◯ Routine ◯ Emergency

Reason for
Visit

Shots

Medication

Other
Treatment

Comments

Vet Visit Log

Date

Age

Kind of Visit   ◯ Routine   ◯ Emergency

Reason for
Visit

Shots

Medication

Other
Treatment

Comments

Pet Details

Photo of Pet

Name
_____

Microchip ID
_____

Species
_____

Breed
_____

Sex
_____

Date of Birth
_____

Color
_____

Markings and
Distinguishing
Features
_____

Responds To
_____

Vaccinations

DATE	AGE	TYPE OF VACCINE	BATCH NUMBER	GIVEN BY	EXPIRES

Vaccinations

DATE	AGE	TYPE OF VACCINE	BATCH NUMBER	GIVEN BY	EXPIRES

Vet Visit Log

Date

Age

Kind of Visit   ◯ Routine   ◯ Emergency

Reason for
Visit

Shots

Medication

Other
Treatment

Comments

Vet Visit Log

Date

Age

Kind of Visit ◯ Routine ◯ Emergency

Reason for
Visit

Shots

Medication

Other
Treatment

Comments

Vet Visit Log

Date

Age

Kind of Visit   ◯ Routine   ◯ Emergency

Reason for
Visit

Shots

Medication

Other
Treatment

Comments

Vet Visit Log

Date

Age

Kind of Visit   ◯ Routine   ◯ Emergency

Reason for
Visit

Shots

Medication

Other
Treatment

Comments

Vet Visit Log

Date

Age

Kind of Visit   ◯ Routine   ◯ Emergency

Reason for
Visit

Shots

Medication

Other
Treatment

Comments

Vet Visit Log

Date

Age

Kind of Visit   ◯ Routine   ◯ Emergency

Reason for
Visit

Shots

Medication

Other
Treatment

Comments

Vet Visit Log

Date

Age

Kind of Visit   ◯ Routine   ◯ Emergency

Reason for
Visit

Shots

Medication

Other
Treatment

Comments

Vet Visit Log

Date

Age

Kind of Visit   ◯ Routine   ◯ Emergency

Reason for
Visit

Shots

Medication

Other
Treatment

Comments

Vet Visit Log

Date

Age

Kind of Visit   ◯ Routine   ◯ Emergency

Reason for
Visit

Shots

Medication

Other
Treatment

Comments

Vet Visit Log

Date

Age

Kind of Visit   ○ Routine   ○ Emergency

Reason for
Visit

Shots

Medication

Other
Treatment

Comments

Vet Visit Log

Date

Age

Kind of Visit   ◯ Routine   ◯ Emergency

Reason for
Visit

Shots

Medication

Other
Treatment

Comments

Vet Visit Log

Date

Age

Kind of Visit   ◯ Routine   ◯ Emergency

Reason for
Visit

Shots

Medication

Other
Treatment

Comments

Vet Visit Log

Date

Age

Kind of Visit   ◯ Routine   ◯ Emergency

Reason for
Visit

Shots

Medication

Other
Treatment

Comments

Vet Visit Log

Date

Age

Kind of Visit   ○ Routine   ○ Emergency

Reason for
Visit

Shots

Medication

Other
Treatment

Comments

Vet Visit Log

Date

Age

Kind of Visit　　○ Routine　　　　○ Emergency

Reason for
Visit

Shots

Medication

Other
Treatment

Comments

Vet Visit Log

Date

Age

Kind of Visit   ◯ Routine   ◯ Emergency

Reason for
Visit

Shots

Medication

Other
Treatment

Comments

Vet Visit Log

Date

Age

Kind of Visit   ◯ Routine   ◯ Emergency

Reason for
Visit

Shots

Medication

Other
Treatment

Comments

Vet Visit Log

Date
_____

Age
_____

Kind of Visit   ◯ Routine   ◯ Emergency
_____

Reason for
Visit

_____

Shots

_____

Medication

_____

Other
Treatment

_____

Comments

Vet Visit Log

Date

Age

Kind of Visit   ○ Routine   ○ Emergency

Reason for
Visit

Shots

Medication

Other
Treatment

Comments

Pet Details

Photo of Pet

Name

Microchip ID

Species

Breed

Sex

Date of Birth

Color

Markings and
Distinguishing
Features

Responds To

Vaccinations

DATE	AGE	TYPE OF VACCINE	BATCH NUMBER	GIVEN BY	EXPIRES

Vaccinations

DATE	AGE	TYPE OF VACCINE	BATCH NUMBER	GIVEN BY	EXPIRES

Vet Visit Log

Date

Age

Kind of Visit   ◯ Routine   ◯ Emergency

Reason for
Visit

Shots

Medication

Other
Treatment

Comments

Vet Visit Log

Date

Age

Kind of Visit   ○ Routine   ○ Emergency

Reason for
Visit

Shots

Medication

Other
Treatment

Comments

Vet Visit Log

Date

Age

Kind of Visit   ◯ Routine   ◯ Emergency

Reason for
Visit

Shots

Medication

Other
Treatment

Comments

Vet Visit Log

Date

Age

Kind of Visit   ◯ Routine   ◯ Emergency

Reason for
Visit

Shots

Medication

Other
Treatment

Comments

Vet Visit Log

Date

Age

Kind of Visit   ◯ Routine   ◯ Emergency

Reason for
Visit

Shots

Medication

Other
Treatment

Comments

Vet Visit Log

Date

Age

Kind of Visit ○ Routine ○ Emergency

Reason for
Visit

Shots

Medication

Other
Treatment

Comments

Vet Visit Log

Date

Age

Kind of Visit   ◯ Routine   ◯ Emergency

Reason for
Visit

Shots

Medication

Other
Treatment

Comments

Vet Visit Log

Date	
Age	
Kind of Visit	◯ Routine ◯ Emergency
Reason for Visit	
Shots	
Medication	
Other Treatment	
Comments	

Vet Visit Log

Date

Age

Kind of Visit   ◯ Routine   ◯ Emergency

Reason for
Visit

Shots

Medication

Other
Treatment

Comments

Vet Visit Log

Date

Age

Kind of Visit   ◯ Routine   ◯ Emergency

Reason for
Visit

Shots

Medication

Other
Treatment

Comments

Vet Visit Log

Date

Age

Kind of Visit   ◯ Routine   ◯ Emergency

Reason for
Visit

Shots

Medication

Other
Treatment

Comments

Vet Visit Log

Date

Age

Kind of Visit   ◯ Routine   ◯ Emergency

Reason for
Visit

Shots

Medication

Other
Treatment

Comments

Vet Visit Log

Date

Age

Kind of Visit   ◯ Routine   ◯ Emergency

Reason for Visit

Shots

Medication

Other Treatment

Comments

Vet Visit Log

Date

Age

Kind of Visit ◯ Routine ◯ Emergency

Reason for
Visit

Shots

Medication

Other
Treatment

Comments

Vet Visit Log

Date

Age

Kind of Visit   ◯ Routine   ◯ Emergency

Reason for
Visit

Shots

Medication

Other
Treatment

Comments

Vet Visit Log

Date

Age

Kind of Visit   ◯   Routine   ◯   Emergency

Reason for
Visit

Shots

Medication

Other
Treatment

Comments

Vet Visit Log

Date

Age

Kind of Visit   ◯ Routine   ◯ Emergency

Reason for
Visit

Shots

Medication

Other
Treatment

Comments

Vet Visit Log

Date

Age

Kind of Visit   ○ Routine   ○ Emergency

Reason for
Visit

Shots

Medication

Other
Treatment

Comments

Vet Visit Log

Date

Age

Kind of Visit   ◯ Routine   ◯ Emergency

Reason for
Visit

Shots

Medication

Other
Treatment

Comments

Notes

Made in the USA
Middletown, DE
07 August 2023

36288706R00066